OCD

And

Nutrition

How Diet Impacts Obsessive-Compulsive Symptoms

Copyright Notice

Disclaimer

This book falls within the realm of nonfiction in the field of health. The information presented here is intended solely for general informational purposes and should not be considered a replacement for professional medical advice, diagnosis, or treatment. It is imperative to always seek guidance from a qualified healthcare provider or physician regarding any inquiries you may have about a medical condition. Please do not disregard professional medical advice or delay seeking it based on the content found in this book.

Contents

Introduction

In the intricate tapestry of mental health, the relationship between nutrition and well-being is a subject of growing interest and significance. As we navigate the complex landscape of mental health conditions, the intersection of diet and mental well-being becomes particularly relevant. "OCD and Nutrition: How Diet Impacts Obsessive-Compulsive Symptoms" invites you to explore this intersection, delving into the nuanced connection between dietary choices and the manifestations of Obsessive-Compulsive Disorder (OCD).

Obsessive-Compulsive Disorder, characterized by persistent intrusive thoughts and repetitive behaviors, presents a unique set of challenges for those affected. While conventional treatments like therapy and medication are essential components, the role of nutrition in influencing OCD symptoms is an emerging area of exploration. In this book, we embark on a journey to unravel the intricate links between diet and the alleviation or exacerbation of obsessive-compulsive symptoms.

This book aims to empower individuals navigating the challenges of OCD to make informed decisions about their dietary choices. From the potential impact of certain nutrients on brain function to the role of gut health in mental well-being,

"OCD and Nutrition" provides a comprehensive exploration of how the food we consume may influence the intricate workings of the mind.

As we embark on this exploration, we recognize that each person's journey with OCD is unique. This book serves as a guide, offering information and practical insights that individuals can incorporate into their holistic approach to managing OCD symptoms. Whether you are personally grappling with OCD, or you are a caregiver seeking to support a loved one, the pages that follow are designed to illuminate the connections between nutrition and mental well-being.

Join me in this exploration of "OCD and

Nutrition," where we navigate the intersection of diet and mental health with a spirit of curiosity, empathy, and the shared goal of enhancing the well-being of those affected by OCD.

Chapter 1

Understanding OCD: Symptoms and Causes

Obsessive-Compulsive Disorder (OCD) is a complex and often debilitating mental health condition that affects millions of people worldwide. It is characterized by recurring, distressing, and intrusive thoughts, known as obsessions, which lead to repetitive and ritualistic behaviors, known as compulsions. This chapter aims to provide an in-depth exploration of OCD, including an overview of the disorder, its symptoms, and the various factors that contribute to its development.

An Overview of Obsessive-Compulsive Disorder

Obsessive-Compulsive Disorder (OCD) is a mental health disorder that falls under the category of anxiety disorders. It typically manifests in two primary components: obsessions and compulsions.

Obsessions

Obsessions are unwanted, distressing, and often irrational thoughts, urges, or mental images that repeatedly enter a person's mind. These thoughts are typically intrusive and cause significant anxiety and discomfort. Common obsessions can include concerns about contamination, fear of harm coming to oneself or others, doubts about completing specific tasks, and a need for order and symmetry.

Compulsions

Compulsions are repetitive, ritualistic behaviors or mental acts performed in response to the obsessions. The purpose of these compulsions is to reduce the distress or anxiety caused by the obsessions. However, these behaviors are often excessive and not connected to any realistic outcome. Compulsions can include actions such as repetitive hand-washing, checking and rechecking locks, counting, and arranging items in specific ways.

OCD can be extremely distressing and time-consuming. Individuals with OCD may find that their daily lives are disrupted by their obsessions and compulsions. This can lead to impaired functioning at work, school, and in social relationships.

Symptoms of OCD

To better understand OCD, it's important to recognize its most common symptoms. These symptoms can vary from person to person, but they typically fall into several categories:

1. **Contamination Obsessions and Cleaning Compulsions:** Individuals with this subtype of OCD are often preoccupied with cleanliness and hygiene. They may constantly fear contamination from germs, dirt, or other harmful substances and engage in excessive cleaning or avoidance behaviors.

2. **Checking Obsessions and Checking Compulsions:** Those with checking OCD frequently worry about leaving doors unlocked, appliances turned on, or other potential safety hazards. They engage in compulsive checking behaviors to alleviate their anxiety.

3. **Symmetry and Order Obsessions and Compulsions:** People with this subtype are fixated on arranging items in specific, symmetrical patterns or maintaining strict order. They may spend an excessive amount of time rearranging objects to achieve perceived symmetry.

4. **Harm Obsessions and Checking or Avoidance Compulsions:** This subtype involves distressing thoughts of causing

harm to oneself or others. Compulsions might include checking to ensure no harm has been done or avoiding situations where harm could occur.

5. **Hoarding:** Hoarding OCD is characterized by the excessive acquisition of items and an inability to discard them, regardless of their value. Hoarding can lead to severely cluttered living spaces.

6. **Pure-O (Pure Obsessional) OCD:** Some individuals experience primarily obsessions without overt compulsions. These obsessions may involve taboo or aggressive thoughts, religious concerns, or other distressing themes.

Factors Contributing to OCD

Understanding the causes of OCD is a complex and ongoing area of research. OCD is believed to result from a combination of genetic, neurological, environmental, and psychological factors. Here are some key factors that contribute to the development of OCD:

1. **Genetic Predisposition:** There is evidence that OCD tends to run in families, suggesting a genetic component. Individuals with a first-degree relative (parent, sibling) with OCD are at a higher risk of developing the disorder themselves.

2. **Brain Structure and Function:** Neuroimaging studies have identified

differences in brain structure and function in individuals with OCD. The basal ganglia, an area of the brain responsible for movement and regulating thought, is thought to play a key role. Dysregulation in serotonin, a neurotransmitter, is also associated with OCD.

3. **Childhood Trauma:** Traumatic experiences during childhood, such as physical or emotional abuse, may increase the risk of developing OCD. Trauma can contribute to the development of anxiety disorders, including OCD.

4. **Stress and Life Transitions:** High levels of stress or significant life changes, such as

starting a new job or experiencing a loss, can trigger the onset of OCD in some individuals.

5. **Infections and Autoimmune Disorders:** In rare cases, certain infections and autoimmune disorders have been linked to the sudden onset of OCD symptoms. This is known as Pediatric Autoimmune Neuropsychiatric Disorders Associated with Streptococcal Infections (PANDAS) and Pediatric Acute-Onset Neuropsychiatric Syndrome (PANS).

6. **Personality Traits:** Certain personality traits, such as perfectionism and high levels of responsibility, may increase the risk of OCD. These traits can predispose individuals to developing obsessions

related to order and cleanliness.

7. **Cognitive and Behavioral Factors:** Maladaptive thought patterns and coping strategies can contribute to the development and maintenance of OCD. For example, individuals may engage in compulsive behaviors as a way to reduce the anxiety associated with obsessions.

8. **Environmental Triggers:** Stressful or traumatic life events can trigger the onset or exacerbation of OCD symptoms. These events can act as a catalyst for the disorder in susceptible individuals.

Obsessive-Compulsive Disorder is a complex and often debilitating mental health condition characterized by distressing obsessions and compulsions. Its symptoms can significantly impact a person's daily life and functioning. The development of OCD is influenced by a combination of genetic, neurological, environmental, and psychological factors. Understanding these factors is crucial for improving diagnosis, treatment, and support for individuals living with OCD.

Chapter 2

Nutrition and Mental Health

In recent years, there has been a growing awareness of the intricate relationship between nutrition and mental health. The food we eat has a profound impact on not only our physical well-being but also our mental and emotional states. Let's now delves into the connection between diet and mental well-being, as well as the specific nutrients that play a vital role in brain function.

The Link between Diet and Mental Well-Being

The adage "you are what you eat" holds more truth than one might initially assume.

Our diet has a direct impact on our mental health and emotional well-being. While the complexities of mental health disorders are multifaceted, it's increasingly clear that nutritional choices can significantly influence the development and management of such conditions. Here are some key aspects of the link between diet and mental well-being:

1. **Mood and Food:** The foods we consume can have a direct impact on our mood. For instance, a diet high in processed foods, sugars, and trans fats has been associated with an increased risk of depression and anxiety. In contrast, diets rich in fruits, vegetables, whole grains, and lean proteins are linked to improved

mental health.

2. **Inflammation and the Brain:** Chronic inflammation is associated with numerous mental health disorders, including depression and anxiety. Consuming an anti-inflammatory diet that is rich in antioxidants and omega-3 fatty acids can help reduce inflammation and potentially alleviate symptoms.

3. **Gut-Brain Connection:** Emerging research has highlighted the importance of the gut-brain axis. The health of our gut microbiome, influenced by our diet, can impact mental health. A balanced diet with sufficient fiber can promote a diverse and healthy gut microbiome, potentially improving mood and cognitive

function.

4. **Nutrient Deficiencies:** Nutrient deficiencies, such as those of vitamins D, B-complex, and omega-3 fatty acids, have been associated with a higher risk of mental health disorders. A well-rounded diet can help prevent these deficiencies and support optimal brain function.

5. **Weight and Body Image:** The relationship between body image, weight, and mental health is complex. Diet and nutrition can affect self-esteem and body image, which, in turn, can impact mental health. It's important to maintain a balanced approach to diet and exercise to support both physical and mental well-being.

Nutrients and Their Impact on Brain Function

Specific nutrients play a crucial role in maintaining and enhancing brain function. Ensuring a well-balanced intake of these nutrients can contribute to better mental health. Here are some key nutrients and their impact on brain function:

1. **Omega-3 Fatty Acids:** Omega-3 fatty acids, particularly eicosapentaenoic acid (EPA) and docosahexaenoic acid (DHA), are essential for brain health. They are found in fatty fish, flaxseeds, and walnuts. Omega-3s are believed to reduce inflammation, support neurotransmitter function, and promote overall brain health.

2. **B Vitamins:** B vitamins, including B6, B9 (folate), and B12, play a crucial role in brain function. They are involved in the synthesis of neurotransmitters like serotonin and dopamine. A deficiency in these vitamins can contribute to depression and other mood disorders. Sources of B vitamins include leafy greens, legumes, and lean proteins.

3. **Vitamin D:** Vitamin D is important for brain development and function. Deficiency has been linked to an increased risk of depression and other mood disorders. Sunlight exposure and fortified foods are common sources of vitamin D.

4. **Antioxidants:** Antioxidants, found in foods like berries, dark chocolate, and green tea, help protect brain cells from oxidative stress. They may also have a neuroprotective effect, potentially reducing the risk of cognitive decline and mood disorders.

5. **Amino Acids:** Amino acids, the building blocks of protein, are essential for the synthesis of neurotransmitters. For example, tryptophan is a precursor to serotonin, which plays a critical role in regulating mood. Protein-rich foods, such as lean meats, dairy, and legumes, provide these amino acids.

6. **Magnesium:** Magnesium is involved in over 300 biochemical reactions in the

body, including those related to brain function. A deficiency in magnesium has been associated with increased anxiety and depression. Foods rich in magnesium include leafy greens, nuts, and whole grains.

7. **Complex Carbohydrates:** Complex carbohydrates, like whole grains and starchy vegetables, provide a steady source of glucose for the brain. This helps maintain stable blood sugar levels and supports cognitive function.

The relationship between nutrition and mental health is an intricate and evolving field of study. What we eat can have a profound impact on our mood, cognitive function, and overall mental well-being. A balanced and nutritious diet, rich in essential nutrients, can contribute to a healthier mind and body. While diet alone cannot be considered a sole treatment for mental health disorders, it is an important element of a holistic approach to mental well-being, working in tandem with other therapeutic strategies, including therapy and medication. As our understanding of this connection deepens, it underscores the importance of adopting a mindful and nutritious diet as an integral part of mental health care.

Chapter 3

The Gut-Brain Connection

In recent years, research has unveiled a remarkable and complex connection between the gut and the brain, often referred to as the "gut-brain connection." This connection underscores the profound influence of the gut microbiome, the community of microorganisms residing in our digestive tract, on our mental health. In this chapter, we'll discuss the role of the gut microbiome in mental health and explore how gut health affects symptoms of Obsessive-Compulsive Disorder (OCD).

The Role of the Gut Microbiome in Mental Health

The human gut is home to trillions of microorganisms, including bacteria, viruses, fungi, and other microbes. This collective community of microorganisms, known as the gut microbiome, plays a pivotal role in maintaining not only our digestive health but also our overall well-being, including mental health. Here are some key aspects of the gut-brain connection:

1. **Neurotransmitter Production:** The gut microbiome is involved in the production of various neurotransmitters, such as serotonin and gamma-aminobutyric acid (GABA). These neurotransmitters are critical for regulating mood, anxiety, and

other aspects of mental health.

2. **Inflammation and Immunity:** An imbalance in the gut microbiome can lead to increased inflammation in the body. Chronic inflammation is associated with various mental health conditions, including depression, anxiety, and even neurodegenerative diseases.

3. **Communication Pathways:** The gut and the brain communicate bidirectionally through the gut-brain axis. This complex network involves various signaling molecules and pathways, allowing the gut to influence the brain and vice versa.

4. **Stress Response:** The gut microbiome can modulate the body's response to stress. Stress, in turn, can have a profound

impact on mental health. Dysregulation
of the gut microbiome may contribute to
an exaggerated stress response.

5. **Immune-Brain Interaction:** The gut
microbiome can influence the immune
system's activity, which, in turn, can
impact brain health. Immune
dysregulation is linked to psychiatric
disorders like schizophrenia and autism.

How Gut Health Affects OCD Symptoms

Obsessive-Compulsive Disorder (OCD) is a
complex mental health condition
characterized by intrusive, distressing
thoughts (obsessions) and repetitive,
ritualistic behaviors (compulsions). While
the exact cause of OCD remains uncertain,

the gut microbiome's role in affecting the severity of OCD symptoms is an emerging area of interest in the scientific community. Here's how gut health can influence OCD:

1. **Inflammation and OCD:** Research suggests that inflammation may play a role in the development and exacerbation of OCD symptoms. An imbalanced gut microbiome can contribute to systemic inflammation, which may, in turn, affect the brain and worsen OCD symptoms.

2. **Neurotransmitters and Obsessions:** As mentioned earlier, the gut microbiome is involved in the production of neurotransmitters, including serotonin. An imbalance in gut bacteria can lead to disruptions in serotonin levels, potentially

exacerbating obsessions and compulsions associated with OCD.

3. **Stress and Gut Microbiome:** Stress is a common trigger for OCD symptoms. The gut microbiome can influence the body's stress response. Dysbiosis in the gut, marked by an imbalance of beneficial and harmful bacteria, can contribute to an exaggerated stress response and potentially exacerbate OCD symptoms.

4. **Gut-Brain Communication:** Communication between the gut and the brain is a two-way street. OCD-related stress and anxiety can disrupt the gut microbiome, and, conversely, gut dysbiosis can send signals to the brain that impact mood and mental health.

5. **Treatment Implications:** Some emerging research suggests that interventions aimed at restoring gut health, such as dietary changes or probiotic supplementation, may be beneficial as a complementary approach to managing OCD. However, more research is needed to establish specific treatment protocols.

The gut-brain connection is a fascinating and evolving field of study that has the potential to shed light on the intricate relationship between the gut microbiome and mental health. The gut microbiome's influence on neurotransmitter production, inflammation, stress response, and immune activity underscores its critical role in mental well-being. For individuals with OCD, understanding and addressing gut health may become an integral part of a holistic approach to managing symptoms. While further research is needed to fully understand the extent of this connection and its therapeutic implications, it offers a promising avenue for improving our understanding and treatment of mental health disorders. As our knowledge deepens, it highlights the importance of a balanced and gut-friendly diet as a key component of mental health care.

Chapter 4

Foods and Substances That Can Worsen OCD

While the exact cause of OCD remains elusive, research has shown that certain foods and substances can exacerbate symptoms, intensify anxiety, and contribute to compulsive behaviors. In this chapter, we will explore the relationship between OCD and trigger foods, with a specific focus on the influence of sugar, caffeine, and processed foods.

Trigger Foods and Compulsive Behavior

OCD symptoms can be exacerbated by a variety of factors, including stress, lack of sleep, and even dietary choices. While food alone is not a direct cause of OCD, certain substances found in various foods can influence mood, anxiety, and brain function, potentially intensifying OCD symptoms. Let's delve into the connection between specific foods and the compulsive behavior associated with OCD:

1. **Sugar and OCD:** Added sugars, particularly in the form of high-fructose corn syrup, can lead to rapid fluctuations in blood sugar levels. These spikes and crashes in blood sugar can cause mood swings, irritability, and increased anxiety. For individuals with OCD, these emotional shifts can intensify the distressing nature of their obsessions and compulsions. In

response to heightened anxiety, they may be more inclined to engage in compulsive behaviors as a way to regain a sense of control.

2. **Caffeine and OCD:** While caffeine can provide a temporary boost in alertness, excessive consumption can lead to restlessness and nervousness. It can also contribute to increased heart rate and exacerbate anxiety. In individuals with OCD, heightened anxiety levels can lead to a compulsion to perform rituals or repetitive behaviors as a way to cope with the intensified stress. Caffeine can disrupt sleep patterns as well, which can be particularly problematic, as inadequate sleep can worsen OCD

symptoms.

3. **Processed Foods and OCD:** Highly processed foods are often devoid of essential nutrients and loaded with artificial additives. The artificial additives in processed foods can negatively affect overall brain function and mood regulation. As a result, individuals with OCD who consume a diet rich in processed foods may experience heightened anxiety and emotional distress, leading to an increase in compulsive behaviors as a coping mechanism.

While food alone is not the primary cause of OCD, certain foods and substances can undoubtedly worsen OCD symptoms and exacerbate compulsive behavior. Understanding the connection between dietary choices and mental health is essential for individuals with OCD and their loved ones. Reducing the consumption of added sugars, moderating caffeine intake, and opting for a diet rich in whole, unprocessed foods can be valuable strategies for managing OCD symptoms. It's important for individuals with OCD to consult with mental health professionals who can provide guidance and support in developing a holistic approach to symptom management, which may include dietary adjustments alongside other treatment modalities like therapy and medication.

Chapter 5

Foods That May Alleviate OCD Symptoms

There's no one-size-fits-all dietary solution for managing OCD. However, emerging research suggests that certain foods and nutrients may play a role in alleviating symptoms. In this chapter, we'll delve into the potential benefits of nutrient-rich diets and the specific impact of omega-3 fatty acids, probiotics, and antioxidants on OCD symptoms.

Nutrient-Rich Diets and Their Potential Benefits

A well-balanced and nutrient-rich diet can have a profound impact on overall health, and emerging evidence suggests that it can also influence mental well-being. For individuals with OCD, adopting a diet rich in essential nutrients may provide several potential benefits:

1. **Neurotransmitter Support:** Nutrient-rich diets can provide the building blocks necessary for the production of neurotransmitters like serotonin, which plays a key role in mood regulation. Adequate levels of serotonin are associated with a reduction in the severity of OCD symptoms.

2. **Inflammation Reduction:** Chronic inflammation is believed to contribute to the development and exacerbation of OCD. Nutrient-dense foods are often anti-

inflammatory and can help reduce inflammation in the body, potentially alleviating symptoms.

3. **Improved Brain Function:** Proper nutrition supports optimal brain function, helping to maintain cognitive health and emotional stability. This can be especially beneficial for individuals with OCD, as cognitive processes play a crucial role in symptom management.

4. **Gut-Brain Axis Health:** The gut-brain axis, which is the connection between the gut and the brain, is influenced by diet. Nutrient-rich foods promote a healthy gut microbiome, which, in turn, can positively impact mental health.

The Impact of Omega-3 Fatty Acids, Probiotics, and Antioxidants

1. **Omega-3 Fatty Acids:** Omega-3 fatty acids, specifically eicosapentaenoic acid (EPA) and docosahexaenoic acid (DHA), are well-known for their brain-boosting properties. These essential fats are found in fatty fish like salmon, mackerel, and walnuts. Omega-3s have anti-inflammatory properties and support the production of serotonin, potentially reducing the severity of OCD symptoms.

2. **Probiotics:** Probiotics are beneficial bacteria that can improve gut health. Emerging research suggests that a balanced gut microbiome is linked to better mental health. Probiotics can help

regulate gut inflammation and reduce overall inflammation, which may alleviate OCD symptoms. Foods like yogurt, kefir, sauerkraut, and kimchi are rich in probiotics.

3. **Antioxidants:** Antioxidants, found in a wide range of fruits, vegetables, and whole grains, help protect brain cells from oxidative stress. These compounds can have a neuroprotective effect, potentially reducing the risk of cognitive decline and mood disorders. Antioxidants also promote overall brain health and may support the management of OCD symptoms.

While diet alone cannot serve as a sole treatment for OCD, adopting a nutrient-rich diet can be an important component of a holistic approach to managing OCD symptoms. Nutrient-rich diets have the potential to support neurotransmitter balance, reduce inflammation, and improve overall brain function. Specific nutrients like omega-3 fatty acids, probiotics, and antioxidants play crucial roles in promoting mental health and may be beneficial for individuals with OCD.

It's important for individuals with OCD to consult with mental health professionals to develop a comprehensive treatment plan that includes dietary considerations alongside therapy and, in some cases, medication. Personalized guidance from healthcare providers, nutritionists, and registered dietitians can help individuals make informed dietary choices that align with their specific needs and goals for managing OCD symptoms.

Chapter 6

Allergies, Sensitivities, and OCD

Obsessive-Compulsive Disorder (OCD) is a multifaceted mental health condition characterized by intrusive thoughts and compulsive behaviors. The origins of OCD are complex and not yet fully understood, but recent research has explored the relationship between food allergies, sensitivities, and OCD. Let's now discuss the exploration of food allergies and sensitivities in relation to OCD and the potential impact of elimination diets on OCD symptoms.

Exploring Food Allergies and Sensitivities in Relation to OCD

While OCD is primarily considered a neurobiological disorder, it's becoming increasingly clear that other factors, including allergies and sensitivities, may influence the severity of its symptoms. Here are key aspects of the connection between food allergies, sensitivities, and OCD:

1. **Inflammation:** Allergies and sensitivities can trigger an inflammatory response in the body. Chronic inflammation has been linked to various mental health disorders, including depression and anxiety. For individuals with OCD, heightened inflammation may exacerbate their symptoms.

2. **Immune Dysregulation:** Allergies and sensitivities often involve an immune system response. Dysregulation of the immune system has been implicated in the onset and severity of OCD, suggesting a potential connection between immune function and the disorder.

3. **Gut-Brain Axis:** The gut-brain axis is the bidirectional communication between the gut and the brain. Emerging research suggests that a disrupted gut microbiome can impact mood and mental health. Food allergies and sensitivities can lead to gut disturbances, potentially affecting OCD symptoms.

4. **Anxiety and Compulsions:** Allergic reactions can trigger anxiety, which, in turn, may exacerbate compulsive behaviors in individuals with OCD. The distress caused by allergies or sensitivities can amplify the emotional turmoil associated with OCD.

5. **Nutrient Deficiencies:** Food allergies or sensitivities may restrict certain food groups from one's diet, potentially leading to nutrient deficiencies. These deficiencies can impact brain health and mood regulation, potentially influencing OCD symptoms.

Elimination Diets and Their Impact on Symptoms

An elimination diet is a structured approach to identify and remove specific foods from one's diet to determine whether they are the source of allergic reactions or sensitivities. The impact of elimination diets on OCD symptoms is a subject of increasing interest. Here's how these diets may affect individuals with OCD:

1. **Identifying Triggers:** An elimination diet can help individuals pinpoint specific foods that trigger allergies or sensitivities. This can be particularly valuable for those with OCD, as removing these triggers may reduce anxiety and emotional distress, potentially leading to

a decrease in compulsive behaviors.

2. **Reducing Inflammation:** By eliminating allergenic foods, individuals may experience a reduction in chronic inflammation. Lower levels of inflammation can benefit individuals with OCD, as chronic inflammation is linked to an exacerbation of symptoms.

3. **Supporting Gut Health:** An elimination diet may contribute to the restoration of a balanced gut microbiome. This can help alleviate gut disturbances associated with allergies and sensitivities, potentially improving mood and overall mental well-being in individuals with OCD.

4. **Nutrient Optimization:** While eliminating specific foods, individuals can focus on

nutrient-dense alternatives, ensuring they meet their nutritional needs. Improved nutrition can support brain health and help manage OCD symptoms.

5. **Psychological Impact:** The process of self-monitoring and observing the effects of an elimination diet can empower individuals with OCD to take control of their dietary choices. This sense of control and accomplishment can positively impact their overall mental well-being.

The connection between food allergies, sensitivities, and OCD is a complex and evolving field of research. While allergies and sensitivities alone may not be the primary cause of OCD, they can influence the severity of symptoms and exacerbate emotional distress. Exploring the potential impact of elimination diets on OCD symptoms is a promising avenue for research and may provide valuable insights into the management of the disorder.

It's crucial for individuals with OCD to consult with mental health professionals and registered dietitians to explore dietary considerations as part of a holistic treatment plan. Personalized guidance, dietary support, and monitoring can help individuals make informed choices and potentially improve their overall well-being in the context of OCD.

Chapter 7

Personalized Nutrition Plans

In the realm of nutrition and well-being, the one-size-fits-all approach no longer suffices. Personalized nutrition plans have emerged as a revolutionary way to address individual dietary needs, taking into account unique factors such as genetics, lifestyle, and health conditions. This chapter explores the concept of personalized nutrition plans, emphasizing the importance of tailoring diets to individual needs and symptoms while working in collaboration with healthcare professionals.

Tailoring Diet to Individual Needs and Symptoms

Personalized nutrition plans are founded on the principle that no two individuals are exactly alike, and what works for one person may not work for another. These plans aim to address specific dietary needs and symptoms, optimizing health and well-being on an individual level. Here are key elements in tailoring diets to individual needs:

1. **Genetic Factors:** Genetic variations can influence how our bodies process and respond to nutrients. Personalized nutrition may involve genetic testing to identify specific genetic traits that affect dietary recommendations. For example,

someone with a genetic predisposition for lactose intolerance may be advised to limit dairy consumption.

2. **Lifestyle and Activity Levels:** An individual's lifestyle and activity levels play a crucial role in determining their nutritional requirements. A person engaged in regular intense physical activity may need a diet with different macronutrient proportions compared to someone with a more sedentary lifestyle.

3. **Health Conditions:** Preexisting health conditions and symptoms can greatly influence dietary recommendations. Individuals with diabetes, for instance, must carefully manage their carbohydrate intake to maintain stable blood sugar

levels. Personalized nutrition plans take such conditions into account, addressing specific dietary considerations.

4. **Food Allergies and Sensitivities:** Identifying and managing food allergies or sensitivities is a crucial aspect of personalized nutrition. For individuals with allergies or sensitivities, a personalized plan will exclude or limit the offending foods to prevent adverse reactions.

5. **Goals and Preferences:** A personalized nutrition plan should align with an individual's dietary preferences and long-term health goals. Whether someone is following a vegetarian or vegan diet, aiming to lose weight, or seeking to build

muscle, the plan should be tailored to support those objectives.

Working with Healthcare Professionals

Creating an effective personalized nutrition plan is not a task that individuals should tackle on their own. Collaborating with healthcare professionals, such as registered dietitians and nutritionists, is essential to ensure that the plan is both safe and effective. Here's why it's crucial to work with healthcare professionals:

1. **Assessment and Evaluation:** Healthcare professionals can conduct comprehensive assessments to understand an individual's dietary habits, health history, and specific needs. This assessment

forms the foundation of a personalized nutrition plan.

2. **Expertise and Knowledge:** Registered dietitians and nutritionists possess the expertise and knowledge needed to navigate complex dietary considerations. They are aware of the latest scientific research, dietary guidelines, and evidence-based strategies for various health conditions.

3. **Tailored Guidance:** Healthcare professionals can provide tailored dietary recommendations based on an individual's unique circumstances. They take into account dietary restrictions, allergies, and preferences, ensuring that the plan is practical and sustainable.

4. **Monitoring and Adjustments:** Personalized nutrition plans are not static; they may need adjustments over time. Healthcare professionals can closely monitor progress, making necessary changes to the plan as health goals evolve or as dietary needs shift.

5. **Accountability and Support:** Healthcare professionals provide a valuable support system. They can offer guidance, answer questions, and motivate individuals to adhere to their personalized nutrition plans, promoting long-term success.

Personalized nutrition plans have ushered in a new era of dietary management, one that acknowledges the importance of individualized approaches to well-being. By tailoring diets to specific needs and symptoms, personalized nutrition plans offer a promising way to optimize health. However, it's essential to recognize that these plans are most effective when developed in collaboration with healthcare professionals who possess the knowledge and expertise needed to create safe, practical, and sustainable dietary recommendations. Working with registered dietitians and nutritionists is the key to unlocking the full potential of personalized nutrition, promoting healthier and more fulfilling lives.

Chapter 8

Lifestyle Changes for OCD Management

Obsessive-Compulsive Disorder (OCD) is a challenging mental health condition that can significantly impact daily life. While treatment often involves therapy and medication, lifestyle changes play a crucial role in managing OCD symptoms. Let's now explore the importance of exercise, sleep, and stress reduction in OCD management and how these lifestyle choices can support dietary improvements to create a holistic approach to well-being.

Exercise, Sleep, and Stress Reduction

1. **Exercise:** Physical activity has been shown to have a positive impact on mental health, including reducing the symptoms of OCD. Exercise releases endorphins, which are natural mood-boosting chemicals, and can help alleviate anxiety and stress. Regular physical activity can also promote better sleep, which is essential for mental health. Incorporating exercise into your daily routine, even in the form of short walks or yoga, can provide benefits.

2. **Sleep:** Sleep is essential for maintaining emotional well-being and cognitive function. Individuals with OCD often struggle with sleep due to racing

thoughts and anxiety. Improving sleep hygiene practices, such as maintaining a regular sleep schedule, creating a comfortable sleep environment, and avoiding stimulants like caffeine close to bedtime, can contribute to better sleep quality, which in turn can help manage OCD symptoms.

3. **Stress Reduction:** Stress is a significant trigger for OCD symptoms. Stress-reduction techniques such as mindfulness, meditation, deep breathing exercises, and progressive muscle relaxation can help individuals with OCD manage their stress levels. These techniques encourage relaxation, reduce the physiological responses to stress, and

may diminish the severity and frequency of obsessions and compulsions.

How Lifestyle Choices Can Support Dietary Improvements

1. **Balanced Diet:** A balanced diet is essential for maintaining overall well-being, and it can have a direct impact on mental health. A diet rich in fruits, vegetables, whole grains, lean proteins, and healthy fats provides essential nutrients that support brain function and mood regulation. By focusing on a balanced diet, individuals with OCD can ensure that their nutritional needs are met, which can aid in symptom management.

2. **Identifying Trigger Foods:** For individuals with OCD who may have food allergies or

sensitivities, avoiding trigger foods can be vital. These trigger foods can exacerbate anxiety, compulsion tendencies, and emotional distress. Identifying and eliminating these foods from the diet can lead to improvements in OCD symptoms.

3. **Nutrient Supplementation:** In some cases, nutrient supplementation may be recommended to address specific deficiencies or imbalances that can affect mental health. Supplements like omega-3 fatty acids, probiotics, and antioxidants may have a beneficial impact on mood and cognitive function, potentially supporting OCD management.

4. **Hydration:** Dehydration can contribute to feelings of restlessness and fatigue, which may intensify OCD symptoms. Maintaining proper hydration is a simple yet often overlooked aspect of well-being that can help individuals feel more balanced and in control.

5. **Meal Timing and Blood Sugar Control:** Some individuals with OCD find that meal timing and blood sugar control can affect their symptoms. Eating regular, balanced meals and snacks can help stabilize blood sugar levels, reducing mood swings and irritability associated with low blood sugar.

Lifestyle changes are integral to managing OCD. Incorporating regular exercise, prioritizing quality sleep, and adopting stress-reduction techniques can alleviate the severity and frequency of OCD symptoms. These changes create a solid foundation for a healthier, more stable emotional state, which complements therapeutic interventions like cognitive-behavioral therapy (CBT) and medication.

Additionally, lifestyle choices that support dietary improvements further contribute to well-being. Maintaining a balanced diet, identifying trigger foods, considering nutrient supplementation, staying hydrated, and focusing on blood sugar control can all enhance the overall effectiveness of OCD management. By recognizing the interplay between lifestyle and mental health, individuals with OCD can proactively take steps to lead healthier, more fulfilling lives.

Chapter 9

Tips for Meal Planning and Grocery Shopping

Meal planning and grocery shopping are cornerstones of a healthy and balanced diet. They provide the structure and discipline needed to make nutritious choices and ensure that you're adequately nourishing your body. In this chapter, we'll explore practical guidance for effective meal planning and grocery shopping to help you achieve a balanced diet.

Why Is Meal Planning Important?

Meal planning offers several advantages, including:

1. **Healthier Food Choices:** Planning your meals in advance allows you to make deliberate and healthier food choices. It helps you avoid impulsive, less nutritious options.

2. **Balanced Nutrition:** By planning meals, you can ensure that your diet includes a variety of foods from all food groups, providing essential nutrients.

3. **Portion Control:** You can manage portion sizes more effectively, preventing overeating and aiding in weight management.

4. **Time and Money Savings:** Meal planning can save time and money by reducing food waste, preventing the need for frequent takeout or dining out,

and making use of cost-effective ingredients.

5. **Reduced Stress:** Knowing what you'll eat in advance can reduce the stress of daily meal decisions.

Practical Tips for Meal Planning

1. **Set Clear Goals:** Define your dietary goals and objectives. Are you aiming for weight loss, muscle gain, or simply maintaining your current weight? Your goals will inform your meal plan.

2. **Choose Balanced Meals:** Include foods from all food groups, including fruits, vegetables, lean proteins, whole grains, and healthy fats, to ensure a balanced diet.

3. **Portion Control:** Use portion control to avoid overeating. You can use measuring cups, a food scale, or visual cues to estimate portion sizes.

4. **Variety is Key:** Don't stick to the same meals every day. Incorporate a wide range of foods to get different nutrients and prevent dietary monotony.

5. **Plan for Snacks:** Include healthy snacks in your meal plan to curb cravings and keep your energy levels stable.

6. **Consider Your Schedule:** Be mindful of your daily routine and plan meals that fit your schedule. Quick and easy meals for busy days, and more elaborate dishes for when you have more time.

7. **Prepare in Advance:** Preparing some components of your meals in advance, like chopping vegetables, can save you time on busy days.

Grocery Shopping Tips

Once you've created your meal plan, grocery shopping is the next step. Consider these tips for effective grocery shopping:

1. **Make a List:** Always make a shopping list based on your meal plan. This helps you stay on track and avoid impulse purchases.

2. **Shop with a Full Stomach:** Shopping when you're hungry can lead to less healthy choices and impulsive purchases.

3. **Read Labels:** Pay attention to food labels,

looking for nutritional information, ingredient lists, and serving sizes.

4. **Buy in Bulk:** Consider buying non-perishable items in bulk, which can be more cost-effective in the long run.

5. **Choose Fresh Produce:** Select a variety of fresh fruits and vegetables, aiming to include a wide range of colors and types for optimal nutrition.

6. **Compare Prices:** Compare prices and consider store brands or generic options to save money.

7. **Avoid Processed Foods:** Minimize the purchase of heavily processed and unhealthy foods, which can be high in sugar, salt, and unhealthy fats.

8. **Check Expiry Dates:** Ensure that perishable items have a reasonable shelf life and won't spoil before you use them.

9. **Limit Impulse Buys:** Stick to your shopping list and avoid unnecessary impulse purchases that can lead to unhealthy eating.

10. **Consider Frozen and Canned Foods:** These options can be just as nutritious as fresh, and they have a longer shelf life.

Effective meal planning and grocery shopping are fundamental to achieving and maintaining a balanced diet. By setting clear goals, choosing balanced meals, practicing portion control, and being mindful of your schedule, you can create a meal plan that aligns with your objectives. When grocery shopping, making a list, shopping with a full stomach, and selecting a variety of fresh, whole foods are essential steps in adhering to your plan and maintaining a healthy diet. With thoughtful planning and strategic shopping, you can nurture your body with the nutrients it needs while optimizing your time and resources.

Chapter 10

Maintaining a Healthy Diet for Long-Term OCD Management

Obsessive-Compulsive Disorder (OCD) often requires a multifaceted treatment approach and diet plays a vital role in long-term OCD management. However, maintaining a healthy diet over time can be a challenging endeavor. In this chapter, we'll explore strategies for sustaining positive dietary habits to support long-term OCD management.

Strategies for Sustaining Positive Dietary Habits

Maintaining a healthy diet for long-term OCD management can be challenging, but the following strategies can help you sustain positive dietary habits:

1. **Set Realistic Goals:** Start with achievable dietary changes. Don't attempt a complete overhaul of your diet all at once. Gradual, sustainable changes are more likely to last.

2. **Seek Professional Guidance:** Consult with a registered dietitian or nutritionist who can help you create a personalized meal plan and provide ongoing support. Professional guidance can be instrumental in sustaining dietary changes.

3. **Keep a Food Journal:** Record your dietary choices and mood in a journal. This can help you identify patterns and make

connections between your diet and OCD symptoms. It also serves as a valuable tool for accountability.

4. **Meal Prepping:** Prepare meals and snacks in advance. Having healthy options readily available can prevent impulsive, less nutritious choices, especially during moments of distress.

5. **Diversify Your Diet:** Embrace a wide variety of foods. Include different fruits, vegetables, whole grains, lean proteins, and healthy fats to ensure you get a broad spectrum of nutrients.

6. **Incorporate Enjoyable Foods:** A healthy diet doesn't mean depriving yourself of foods you enjoy. Include your favorite foods in moderation to maintain

satisfaction with your dietary choices.

7. **Social Support:** Share your dietary goals with friends and family, or consider involving a loved one in your dietary journey. Social support can help you stay motivated and accountable.

8. **Mindful Eating:** Practice mindful eating by paying attention to hunger and fullness cues. This can prevent overeating and help you savor your food.

9. **Celebrate Small Wins:** Acknowledge and celebrate your successes, no matter how minor they may seem. Small accomplishments can provide motivation to continue making positive dietary choices.

10. **Mind-Body Techniques:** Incorporate relaxation techniques like meditation, deep breathing, or yoga to manage stress and reduce emotional eating tendencies.

11. **Frequent Check-Ins:** Periodically reassess your dietary habits and their impact on your OCD symptoms. Adjust your approach as needed to better suit your evolving needs.

12. **Forgive Slip-Ups:** Understand that maintaining a healthy diet is a journey with occasional detours. Don't be too hard on yourself for slip-ups; instead, use them as learning experiences to improve.

Maintaining a healthy diet for long-term OCD management is an ongoing process that requires commitment and patience. By setting realistic goals, seeking professional guidance, and using strategies like meal prepping, mindful eating, and social support, you can establish and sustain positive dietary habits. Remember that a healthy diet is just one aspect of comprehensive OCD management, and it should be part of a holistic approach that includes therapy, medication, and other necessary interventions. With determination and a supportive environment, sustaining a balanced diet can contribute to better long-term OCD management and overall well-being.

Chapter 11

Research and Future Directions

Obsessive-Compulsive Disorder (OCD) is a complex mental health condition characterized by intrusive thoughts and compulsive behaviors. While research on the relationship between nutrition and OCD is ongoing, the field has seen significant advancements in recent years. In this chapter, we will delve into the current studies and ongoing research in the field of OCD and nutrition, as well as the potential advances on the horizon.

Current Studies and Ongoing Research in the Field

1. **Nutritional Psychiatry:** Nutritional psychiatry is a burgeoning field that investigates the impact of diet on mental health. Researchers are conducting studies to examine the role of various nutrients, such as omega-3 fatty acids, probiotics, antioxidants, and certain vitamins and minerals, in the management of OCD symptoms.

2. **Gut-Brain Axis:** The gut-brain axis is a topic of increasing interest. Research is exploring how the gut microbiome influences mental health, including the onset and severity of OCD. Ongoing studies are investigating the use of

probiotics and dietary interventions to modulate the gut microbiome and potentially alleviate OCD symptoms.

3. **Inflammation and Immune System:** Chronic inflammation and immune system dysregulation are associated with OCD. Researchers are examining the impact of anti-inflammatory diets and dietary supplements in reducing inflammation and potentially improving OCD symptoms.

4. **Food Allergies and Sensitivities:** Food allergies and sensitivities have gained attention for their potential role in exacerbating OCD symptoms. Ongoing research is aimed at better understanding how specific foods or food components

may trigger OCD symptoms in susceptible individuals.

5. **Genetic and Epigenetic Factors:** Genetic and epigenetic research is shedding light on how an individual's genetic makeup and gene expression may influence their susceptibility to OCD and their response to dietary interventions. Studies in this area are expected to uncover potential personalized dietary approaches for OCD management.

6. **Dietary Patterns and Mental Health:** Researchers are examining the impact of overall dietary patterns, such as the Mediterranean diet and the DASH diet, on mental health, including OCD. These diets, which emphasize whole foods,

fruits, vegetables, and healthy fats, have shown promise in improving mood and may have implications for OCD management.

Potential Advances in OCD and Nutrition

1. **Personalized Nutrition:** The future of OCD management may involve personalized nutrition plans that consider an individual's genetic, dietary, and gut microbiome factors. These plans would provide tailored dietary recommendations to address specific OCD symptoms and triggers.

2. **Targeted Dietary Interventions:** Researchers are exploring the development of targeted dietary

interventions for OCD. These interventions could involve specific nutrient supplementation, dietary restrictions, or the incorporation of foods rich in particular nutrients known to influence brain health and mood.

3. **Integration of Nutritional and Psychological Approaches:** Future approaches to OCD management may involve the integration of nutritional interventions with existing psychological treatments, such as cognitive-behavioral therapy (CBT). Combining these modalities could provide a more comprehensive and effective treatment strategy.

4. **Advanced Gut Microbiome Manipulation:**
As our understanding of the gut-brain
axis grows, so too may our ability to
manipulate the gut microbiome for
therapeutic purposes. Future research
may lead to more targeted and effective
interventions to address OCD through
microbiome modulation.

5. **Epigenetic Therapies:** Epigenetic
research may lead to the development of
epigenetic therapies that can modify
gene expression related to OCD.
Nutritional approaches that influence
gene regulation could be an exciting
avenue for future research and
treatment.

6. **Big Data and AI:** The use of big data and artificial intelligence (AI) is expected to play a significant role in advancing our understanding of the relationship between nutrition and OCD. Analyzing large datasets can reveal complex patterns and potential treatment strategies.

The intersection of OCD and nutrition is a dynamic and evolving field of research. Ongoing studies and future directions hold promise for personalized nutrition plans, targeted interventions, and the integration of nutritional and psychological approaches to OCD management. As our knowledge of the gut-brain axis, genetics, and epigenetics expands, we can anticipate more sophisticated and effective strategies for the management of OCD, ultimately improving the lives of individuals affected by this condition.

Conclusion

As we conclude our exploration into the intricate relationship between nutrition and Obsessive-Compulsive Disorder (OCD), we reflect on the profound impact that dietary choices can have on mental well-being. "OCD and Nutrition: How Diet Impacts Obsessive-Compulsive Symptoms" has been a journey through the evolving landscape of mental health, where the interplay between what we consume and the manifestations of OCD becomes increasingly apparent.

In these pages, we've delved into the potential influence of nutrients on brain function, the role of gut health in mental well-being, and the broader context of lifestyle choices that may contribute to either the exacerbation or alleviation of OCD symptoms. It is crucial to recognize that this exploration is not a panacea but an empowering addition to the toolkit of individuals grappling with OCD and those supporting them.

As we embrace the complexities of each person's unique journey, we encourage readers to approach the information provided with an open mind, recognizing the individuality of responses to dietary interventions. The intent of this book is not to prescribe rigid dietary regimens but to inspire informed decision-making and a holistic approach to mental health.

In the spirit of ongoing discovery and

personal empowerment, we acknowledge that the field of nutritional psychiatry is ever-evolving. This book serves as a stepping stone, inviting readers to engage in a continued exploration of the dynamic connections between nutrition, mental well-being, and the management of OCD symptoms.

May the insights shared within these pages contribute to a greater understanding of the intricate relationship between diet and mental health. Whether you are an individual navigating your personal journey with OCD or a caregiver seeking ways to support a loved one, may this book inspire a thoughtful and informed approach to incorporating nutritional considerations into the broader landscape of mental well-being.

As we move forward, let us embrace the power of knowledge, empathy, and personalized care in the quest for holistic well-being. May this book serve as a catalyst for continued exploration, fostering a sense of empowerment and resilience for those on the path to managing and understanding OCD through the lens of nutrition.